ILLUSTRATIONS OF OLD TESTAMENT HISTORY

ILLUSTRATIONS OF
OLD TESTAMENT HISTORY

BY

R. D. BARNETT

PUBLISHED BY

The Trustees of the British Museum

LONDON

PRINTED IN ENGLAND BY
HAZELL WATSON AND VINEY LTD
AYLESBURY, BUCKS

CONTENTS

Foreword		*page* 7
1	The Babylonian Legend of the Flood	9
2	The 'Amarna Letters' and the Cities of Canaan	12
3	Hazor and the Conquests of Joshua	16
4	The Philistines	24
5	Canaanite Cult Figures	32
6	The Wisdom of Amenemope	34
7	Passing Children through the Fire of Moloch	37
8	Phoenician Tribute	39
9	The Ivory House of Ahab	42
10	Cherubim and the Temple of Solomon	44
11	Shalmaneser III (859–824 B.C.)	46
12	The Homage of Jehu	48
13	Tiglath-Pileser III Invades Palestine	50
14	The Capture of Samaria (722 B.C.)	52
15	Sennacherib and Hezekiah	56
16	The Siege of Lachish	60
17	The Tomb of Shebna, a Royal Steward	66
18	The Lachish Letters	68
19	The End of Assyria, the Fall of Nineveh, and the Capture of Jerusalem	70
20	The Accession of Cyrus the Mede	76
21	Darius, the Great King, and the Palace of Shushan	78
22	The Dead Sea Scrolls	80
23	Reminiscences of the Temple of Herod: The Ossuary of Nicanor	83
Bibliography		87

FOREWORD

THE study of that portion of the Bible called the Old Testament, both in its original tongue and in translation, has long been one of the most proudly cherished traditions of the English-speaking peoples. The close investigation of the Holy Land, the study of its sites and surviving ancient monuments and all matters found in it that furnish a better understanding of the Bible are, of course, a more recent development, since Near Eastern Archaeology (outside Egypt) is of but recent growth as a whole. Starting only from the time of the great Assyrian discoveries of Layard and Botta and their successors in the forties of the last century, it was much developed in Palestine by the Palestine Exploration Fund (founded in 1865) and the German Palästina-Verein (founded in 1877). But thanks to this great tradition of study and research, we are in this country extremely fortunate to have been able to assemble over the years, and thereby preserve in this Museum a remarkable number of items from various sources throwing a direct light on the historical events mirrored in the pages of the Hebrew Bible. They are, of course, only a portion of all the material of this kind which exists, much being found in museums in other countries, which the student of the subject will find described elsewhere.

In this booklet we attempt to relate the selection of material more or less to particular historical events. The relation has not been absolutely strict. Such matters of selection are inevitably difficult, and in the last resort, depend on personal preferences. But we have avoided here trying to show everything which can illustrate the ancient background of the Bible. All will agree that, if we wish to illustrate the background of the sojourn of the Children of Israel in Egypt, we should refer to a large part of the collections of the Department of Egyptian Antiquities; and similarly, if we wish to illustrate as a similar background, the life and beliefs of the Israelites' neighbours, the Assyrians and Babylonians, the Department of Western Asiatic Antiquities will serve this purpose as a whole, for it largely consists of illustrations of those peoples' civilisations. In fact, we have not even brought in other types of Palestinian material remains, which show only in general ways the daily life of the Israelites, since such do not really fall under the definition of illustrating history. In one case, however, we have slightly broadened our definition, to illustrate with material from Palestine and Carthage (items 5, 7, 10) the pagan worship against which the prophets and lawgivers of Israel long struggled. And, for completeness' sake, we have slightly extended the series in time to the period of the destruction of the Second Temple, although, strictly speaking, that is already beyond the events described in the books of the Old Testament. Those who desire to follow the subject of historical illustration further with the aid of ancient Palestinian coins, should consult the resources of the Department of Coins and Medals. The material described here is all preserved in the Department of Western Asiatic Antiquities, with one exception—the Egyptian papyrus of Amenemope, which is in the Department of Egyptian Antiquities. It is of such interest and importance that a description of it by Mr. T. G. H. James is included, by courtesy of the Keeper of that Department.

R. D. BARNETT

I. THE BABYLONIAN LEGEND OF THE FLOOD

BETWEEN 1845 and 1851, a young Englishman, Austen Henry Layard, discovered the palaces of the Assyrian Kings at their capitals of Nimrud (the Biblical Calah: Genesis x) and Kuyunjik (ancient Nineveh), the latter being just outside Mosul. Sculptures from these palaces are to be seen on the ground floor. At Kuyunjik two libraries of clay tablets, inscribed in the cuneiform (wedge-shaped) writing, were found by Layard in the Palace of Sennacherib and by Rassam in the Palace of Ashurbanipal. A period followed in which this method of writing on these tablets and other inscriptions was gradually deciphered and the tablets of the Royal Library at Nineveh, having been brought back to the British Museum, were gradually classified and arranged. In 1872, George Smith, an Assistant in the Department of Antiquities, gifted with a genius for decipherment, announced that he had discovered on one of these a version of the story of the Deluge which very closely resembled that in the Book of Genesis. Unfortunately the tablet was incomplete. The announcement created such public interest that the *Daily Telegraph* offered to pay £1,000 for the expenses if the Trustees would send out Smith to reopen the excavations and try to find the missing portions. The offer was accepted. Smith went out to Kuyunjik, and, despite his complete inexperience of excavation, returned triumphant with, among other discoveries, a missing portion. But his success had a tragic conclusion. The public having insisted on his return for a further season to Mesopotamia, he did so, but it proved fruitless, and he died of fever on the way home.

The Flood Legend discovered by Smith was a late Assyrian version of the tale. It was known to the Babylonians in the 18th century B.C., and before them to the Sumerians. The Assyrian version is preserved as an interpolation at the end of another much longer poem, called the poem of Gilgamesh, of which it forms the XIth tablet. Gilgamesh is seeking a means which will restore his dead friend Enkidu to life, and finds Utnapishtim, who recites to him how he had obtained eternal life, though a mortal. Mankind had angered the Storm-god Enlil who decided to drown them all with a mighty flood. Ea, the god of wisdom, took pity on one man, Utnapishtim, and whispered a warning to the reed-hut in which Utnapishtim dwelt. The reeds warned him, and he prepared his escape and that of his family by taking them and other living things into a great ark. When the rains descended, mankind was destroyed. After six days, the waters sank, and the ship touched ground. A bird was released, and 'flew to and fro, but found no resting-place'.

Then a swallow was sent out, but returned; finally, a raven was released but did not return, showing the water had sunk and revealed land. Utnapishtim thereupon disembarked and sacrificed to the gods, who, though angry at his escape, were persuaded to grant him divine honours and a dwelling-place at the mouth of the River Euphrates.

FIG. 1—K3375. Clay Tablet from Kuyunjik inscribed with part of Babylonian Legend of the Flood. Size 15·5 cm. × 13·8 cm. *Room of Writing.*

The story follows the lines of that of Noah closely, though there are distinct differences, the most noticeable being the polytheism of the Mesopotamian account. Yet clearly there was some point of contact between the two legends. The manner and date at which this legend became first known to the Hebrews is not fully agreed. But these portions of the cuneiform literature of Babylonia were certainly known to and read by Phoenician and Syrian scribes and scholars by the 15th century B.C. Perhaps the contact belongs, as some think, to the period when the Jews were themselves carried into captivity (8th–6th century B.C.).

The still incomplete tablet found by Smith was later duplicated and completed by others found elsewhere.

It may be noted that the Sumerians believed that a Great Flood had occurred at a very remote period of their history.

In the course of the excavations which C. L. Woolley (later Sir Leonard Woolley) conducted at the site of Ur of the Chaldees, he made a number of deep soundings, mostly in the 'Royal Cemetery' area, to the base of the mound at sea level. In several of these, he found a layer of sterile clay of a thickness varying from less than 1 to over 3·5 metres. Both above and below this layer were remains of painted prehistoric pottery in the Ubaid style, probably to be dated between about 4000 and 3500 B.C., and human female figurines with stylised faces. Woolley believed that he had discovered evidence of the Great Flood described in Sumerian and Biblical legend, but this interpretation was not by any means universally accepted, and indeed was very seriously doubted.

Similar sterile levels had been found at other sites in Babylonia, though not at the same period. Nevertheless, these observations made it highly probable that this stratum was deposited at Ur by unusually severe annual inundations of merely local extent.

In a survey of the evidence at Ur and other sites, Professor M. E. L. Mallowan has recently come to the conclusion that the Deluge in Babylonia which the Epic of the Flood describes, was a genuinely historical event, traces of which have been discovered in the excavations of Tell Fara, (the ancient Shuruppak, home of Ziusudra the Sumerian equivalent of Utnapishtim), and perhaps at Kish, but not at Ur.

2. THE 'AMARNA LETTERS' AND THE CITIES OF CANAAN

IN about 1380 B.C., a youthful Pharaoh ascended the throne of Egypt under the name of Amenhotep (Greek authors render it as Amenophis), the fourth of that name. A courageous original thinker of genius, he set himself to reform the established Egyptian religious pattern of worship by dethroning the whole elaborate (Egyptian) pantheon in favour of the worship of only one deity, the disk of the sun, the Aten of Ra. He changed his own name to Akhen-aten, moved the capital from Thebes to the site Akhetaten, now called Tell-el-Amarna, in Middle Egypt, and carried out a reformation of Egyptian art in his new capital. While this was taking place, the Egyptian empire in Palestine and Syria was utterly neglected. The Hittites, a newly-arisen power on their northern frontiers, led by able and ambitious monarchs, steadily spread their control further southwards by intrigue or force or bribery.

At Tell-el-Amarna in 1887, the remarkable discovery was made of a great collection of clay tablets, inscribed (strangely enough, for a find made in Egypt!), in cuneiform script, and written in the Babylonian language, which was evidently the lingua franca of the day used for political and diplomatic purposes, much as French is today. These tablets were the diplomatic archives from the Foreign Office of Amenhotep IV, alias Akhen-aten, and his father Amenhotep III dealing with the affairs of the North, i.e. Syria, Phoenicia, Babylonia, the Mitanni and the Hittites. Many of the letters from this archive are in the British Museum, others are in Berlin and elsewhere. They are of particular interest in telling us of the state of Palestine at a period before the reputed date of the Hebrews' Exodus from Egypt. Many are addressed from cities known to us at a later date. But at this date, they are Canaanite vassals of Amenhotep IV, whose help they implore against his enemies. While he dreamed his dreams of religious reform, they implored in vain, and most of the Empire in Syria and Palestine was lost eventually to Egypt. In many of these tablets, a class of marauders called Habiru is mentioned who, by some scholars, have been equated with the Hebrews (Heb. *'ibri*) but this is not by any means certain, or widely accepted. The following are some examples of these documents:

B.M. 29830 *Letter No. 47:* (EA No. 227) Letter from 'Abdi-tirshi, the ruler of Hazor, to the king of Egypt, assuring him that he will guard the king's cities, and expressing his joy at the arrival of a message from the king.

12

29844

29835

29832

Fig. 2—Letters in cuneiform from Tell-el-Amarna. Scale 1 : 1

29831   *Letter No. 48:* (EA No. 228) Letter from 'Abdi-tirshi, ruler of Hazor, to the king expressing his loyalty and drawing his lord's attention to the good care he has taken of the cities in his charge.

29832   *Letter No. 49:* (EA No. 299) Letter from Yapahi, ruler of Gezer, acknowledging the receipt of a message from the king and asking for assistance against the Habiru.

29835   *Letter No. 52:* (EA No. 325) Letter from Widiya, governor of Ashkelon, to the king, stating that he is guarding the cities entrusted to him, and also that he has prepared the provisions required from him as well as the tribute.

29840   *Letter No. 57:* (EA No. 296) Letter from Yahtiri, governor of Gaza and Joppa, assuring the king of his loyalty, recalling the fact that he was brought up at the Egyptian court and that 'the yoke of the king, my lord, is on my neck and I am bearing it.' *Room of Writing.*

29844   *Letter No. 61:* Translation: *ANET*, p. 486 (EA No. 252.) Letter from Labaya, prince of Shechem, explaining the capture of a certain town and refuting slanders which have reached the king. Labaya quotes a proverb, 'If ants are smitten, they do not acquiesce but they bite the hand of the man who strikes them', to justify action he had taken.

29848   *Letter No. 65:* (EA No. 330) Letter from Shipti-ba'al of Lachish assuring the king that he and Yanhamu are loyal and faithful servants.

29851   *Letter No. 68:* (EA No. 282) Letter from Shuwardata, prince of Hebron, telling the king that he stands alone and needs a large force to rescue him.

29855   *Letter No. 72:* Translation: *ANET*, p. 485 (EA No. 245). Second part of a letter from Biridiya of Megiddo, accusing Zurata of Accho of treachery.

29855

29851

29848

Fig. 3—Letters in cuneiform from Tell-el-Amarna. Scale 1 : 1

3. HAZOR AND THE CONQUESTS OF JOSHUA

'TELL' is an Arabic word meaning an artificial mound created by successive layers of habitations superimposed one upon the other, usually implying great antiquity. Tell-el-Qedah, 5 miles SW. of Lake Huleh, north of Galilee is one of these. It covers more than 20 acres with an average width of 200 metres. Its slopes rise 40 metres above the surrounding plain. This site was identified by the late Professor John Garstang in 1928 as the site of the lost Canaanite city of Hazor, the principal city of the Canaanites of Northern Palestine, which the 'Children of Israel', led by Joshua, were said to have captured soon after their entry into the Promised Land:

> and Joshua at that time turned back and took Hazor, and smote the king thereof with the sword; for Hazor before time was the head of all those Kingdoms . . . and he burnt Hazor with fire. (Joshua xi. 10–11).

In 1955–8 a team of archaeologists from the Hebrew University of Jerusalem, under the leadership of Professor Yigael Yadin, supported by the late James A. de Rothschild and others, excavated the site of Tell-el-Qedah. Though no absolute proof was found to confirm its identification as Hazor, there is hardly any reason to doubt it; the evidence from the excavations, in fact, coincides remarkably with the Biblical record. Excavation produced proofs of nine occupation levels of the Bronze Age or Canaanite period. During the last five of these the occupation also extended to an area of about 150 acres to the north of the Tell, known as the 'Lower City.'

In the SW corner of the lower City were found Canaanite houses, their floors littered with pottery of the 13th century B.C. (the late Bronze Age), some local, some imported from Cyprus and the Greek lands, called Mycenaean ware. This pottery is well known, and can be closely dated. The city level of which these houses formed part belonged to the 13th century B.C., and showed signs of violent destruction and abandonment. This now fits excellently with the tradition of its capture by Joshua after the Exodus dated by many scholars to the late 13th century B.C.

The level below this final Bronze Age city corresponded to the 14th century B.C.—the period of the Amarna letters. Two of the letters found at El-Amarna had in fact been written by the ruler of Hazor. (See above, No. 2, B.M. 29830 and 29831).

These excavations provided proof of the existence of a large Canaanite

16

FIG. 4—Pottery of the 14th century B.C. (late Bronze Age IIA), from Hazor.

city extending all over the enclosure, with a population estimated to have numbered perhaps 40,000 people. In these areas were found notably a temple of the Sun-god and a temple of the Moon-god.

In the highest part of the tell, was the citadel. Here were found remains of the Israelite town, covering 300 years from Solomon to Pekah. The uppermost Israelite level belonged to the kings of the period of Jeroboam II (786–746 B.C.), but was destroyed by the invasion of Tiglath-pileser in 732 B.C. Below this was a Stratum belonging to the reign of Ahab, *c.* 850 B.C. Later rebuilding continued into Hellenistic times.

The figures show pottery from Hazor presented by C. Clore, Esq., and the Anglo-Israel Archaeological Society.

Fig. 5—Storage jar of the 14th century B.C. (late Bronze Age IIA), from Hazor. Height 1·03 m.

FIG. 6—Pottery of the 13th century B.C. (late Bronze Age IIB), the time of the Exodus and the Conquest. Right, Cypriot jug; left and top, Mycenaean pilgrim flask and stirrup jar. From Hazor.

FIG. 7—Pot and stand of the 9th–8th centuries B.C., the time
of the early Israelite Monarchy. From Hazor. Height 76 cm.

FIG. 8—Pottery of the early 8th century B.C., the time of Joash and Jeroboam II. From Hazor.

22

Fig. 9—Pottery of the late 8th century B.C., the time of Menahem and Pekah. From Hazor.

23

4. THE PHILISTINES

THE fall and sack of the great city of Troy in NW. Turkey, possibly before 1200 B.C., is thought to have been the signal for the collapse of the Hittite Empire which till then had ruled most of the land mass of Asia Minor. The Hittite capital was destroyed while a mixed army of assailants and freebooters from the Aegean shores and hinterland swept on southwards through Syria and Palestine, leaving a trail of burnt and ravaged cities in their wake. According to Egyptian sources, among the leaders of this force (whom they called the 'Peoples of the Sea') were Achaeans (Greeks, of the time of Homer's epics), and particularly the Philistines. In the 8th year of the Pharaoh, Rameses III, this wave of sea and land-raiders reached the north-eastern (Sinai) frontier of Egypt, but were at last defeated and thrown back; the Philistines were, however, strong enough to settle where they were stayed by the Egyptians on the Shephelah, the coastal plain of SW. Palestine, which has borne their name (derived from *Pelashet, Pelishti =* Philistia, Philistine, since then extended to the whole country) until modern times. The Philistines are represented in the Egyptian temple reliefs as wearing, for war purposes, a curious corselet and kilt with tassels, and a headdress with a thick, stiff encircling crest like a crown, more likely made of horsehair (see casts, Figs. 10–12), than as is often suggested, of feathers.

The history of the Philistines' conflict with the Hebrews during the next two centuries is described in the Old Testament (Judges, Samuel) and is well known. Actual remains of the Philistines are rather scanty. In Palestine, their cultural remains have been found, chiefly in the form of a peculiar polychrome pottery (derived from Greek Late Mycenaean III c. ware), painted in reds and browns on a white slip with loop or bird designs (see fragments from Beth Shemesh in Fig. 13). In a few instances, however, burials of individuals, probably soldiers, have been found in clay coffins with a detachable lid, bearing a very crude representation of the dead man. Such Philistine coffins have been found at Bethshan and Tell Farah in Palestine; similar ones come from frontier sites in Egypt, where the deceased had apparently served the Pharaoh as mercenaries. One such coffin lid found in Egypt is shown here from Tell Yahudiyeh (Fig. 15); another from Nebesheh is in the Department of Egyptian Antiquities. Both were excavated by the late Sir Flinders Petrie.

Very closely associated with the Philistines among the 'Peoples of the Sea' was another military race called Shardana or Sherden, who are

FIG. 10—Plaster casts of heads of Philistine soldiers represented at Thebes, Egypt. Presented by the late Sir Flinders Petrie. 12th century B.C. Height 25 cm.

FIG. 11—Plaster casts of heads of Philistine soldiers represented at Thebes, Egypt. Presented by the late Sir Flinders Petrie. 12th century B.C. Height 31 cm.

FIG. 12—Plaster casts of heads of Philistine soldiers represented at Thebes, Egypt. Presented by the late Sir Flinders Petrie. 12th century B.C. Height 35 cm.

Fig. 13—Fragments of Philistine pottery. From Beth Shemesh (Ain Shems).

represented on Egyptian reliefs wearing a curious horned helmet and armed with a round shield, and a huge bronze broadsword, larger than any others of that date. A unique example of these swords found at a village called Beit Dagin, near Tel-Aviv, Israel, is in the British Museum (Fig. 16).

FIG. 14—Philistine jug with strainer mouth (partly restored). From Tell-Farah, near Gaza. Height 25 cm × diameter 17·5 cm.

Fig. 15—127386. Coffin lid of a Philistine. From Tell Yahudiyeh.
(Presented by the Egyptian Exploration Fund.) Height 49 cm.

FIG. 16—127137.   Bronze Shardana broadsword from Beit Dagin, near
Jaffa-Tel-Aviv. Length 1·07 m. *Syrian Room.*

5. CANAANITE CULT FIGURES

THE heathen neighbours of the Hebrews in ancient Palestine practised a nature-religion in which the all-important powers of fertility and the atmosphere were imagined in visible form and worshipped in rites which the Hebrews found idolatrous, loathsome and often cruel. Among those commonly represented in Palestine were figurines in baked clay representing the Canaanite mother-goddess holding her breasts (Fig. 17(a)). Her exact identity is unestablished, but she may represent either Ashtart (vocalised as Ashtaroth in the Old Testament), or Anath, or both. Such figures are found in ancient houses or graves of the Early Iron Age. The present figure is said to have been found with a small perfume vase, jug, and a green stone pendant, probably the equipment of a woman's grave. Against the use of such fertility figures as this the second Commandment was addressed and the Prophets struggled.

A curious cult-figure, with two heads very crudely indicated, has a cavity seemingly for inserting some offering, perhaps seeds of some plant, or incense or some other symbol of sacrifice (Fig. 17(b)).

FIG. 17(a) 93091. Reddish clay, with traces of whitish paint.
Height: 17·5 cm.
Width: 7·6 cm.
From a grave near 'Rachel's Tomb', Bethlehem.

FIG. 17(b) 59196. Reddish clay.
Presented by Miss B. Tickell.
Height: 10·4 cm.
Width: 8·5 cm.

6. THE WISDOM OF AMENEMOPE

THE text known as the *Wisdom of Amenemope* is preserved completely on a papyrus 1·70 m. in length, in the Department of Egyptian Antiquities. It is a didactic composition of a type very popular in Egypt from the time of the early Middle Kingdom (about 2000 B.C.). The common formula employed is that of a wise man speaking to his son, handing on knowledge of life and the ways of good behaviour that he has found proper in his own life. This work, entitled *Teaching how to live and guidance for welfare* . . . was supposedly composed by the official Amenemope, son of Kanakhte, for his son Harmakheru. The date of its actual composition is not known, but it is thought by some to have been about 1250 B.C.; the document in which the text is preserved was written by the scribe Senu at a much later date, possibly about 750 B.C.

Ever since it was first published by Sir Wallis Budge in 1922, *Amenemope* has received almost as much critical attention from Biblical scholars as from Egyptologists, the reason being that many of the sayings and precepts voiced by the wise Egyptian official can be paired with sayings in the Book of Proverbs.

Amenemope says:	The writer of Proverbs says:
Give thine ears, hear what is said, give thy mind to interpret them; to put them in your heart is good.	*Bow down thine ear and hear the words of the wise and apply thine heart unto my knowledge* (xxii. 17).

An even closer parallel exists between what *Amenemope* and the writer of Proverbs have to say about the angry man:

Amenemope says:	The writer of Proverbs says:
Do not associate with the angry man nor approach him for conversation. . . . Do not leap to join such a man lest a terror carry thee away.	*Make no friendship with an angry man; and with a furious man thou shall not go; lest thou learn his ways and get a snare to thy soul.* (Proverbs xxii. 24–5).
Better is poverty at the hand of god than riches in the storehouse.	*Better is little with the fear of the Lord, than great treasure, and trouble therewith.*

Many other verbal parallels exist between the two compositions, and they contain even more parallels of meaning. The similar passages are conveniently set out side by side in the article by D. C. Simpson quoted below. At first it was thought that much of Proverbs was based directly on the *Wisdom of Amenemope*. Subsequently the critical pendulum

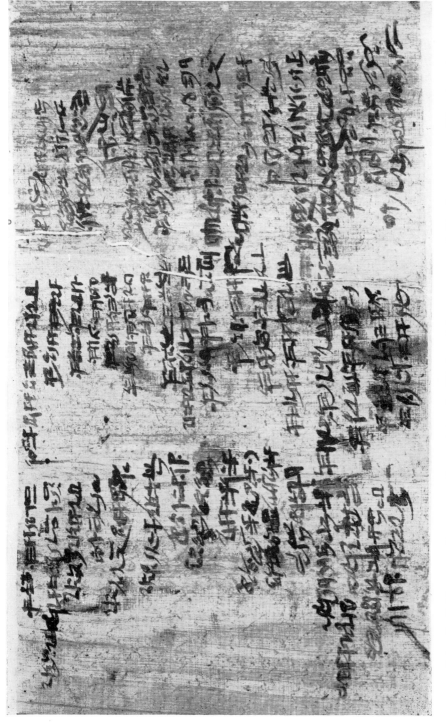

FIG. 18—B.M. 10474: Papyrus scroll containing the *Wisdom of Amenemope*; probably about 750 B.C. Hieratic script. *Third Egyptian Room.*

swung the other way and some scholars maintained that *Amenemope* was based on Proverbs.   Others considered that both texts derived from a common source, probably written in a Semitic language. It is possible, however, that the close relationship may be explained simply on the ground that both were composed with the same intellectual background. Didactic works of this kind were common throughout the ancient East and much of the contents of *Proverbs* and of *Amenemope* is made up of the commonplaces of popular wisdom.

7. PASSING CHILDREN THROUGH THE FIRE OF MOLOCH

For the children of Judah have done that which is evil in My sight, saith the Lord ... and they have built the high places of Topheth which is in the valley of the son of Hinnom, to burn their sons and their daughters in the fire, which I commanded not, neither came it into my mind. (Jeremiah VII. 30–31.)

IN their fierce denunciations of the practice of Canaanite nature religions, the authors of various books of the Old Testament make several attacks on the forbidden custom of 'passing the children through the fire to Moloch' (e.g. Leviticus xviii. 21, xx, 2–5; 2 Kings xxiii. 10). It may be assumed that this name, connected with the root *mlk* 'to rule', is in fact a version of the name, or, more accurately, the title of a Canaanite or Phoenician deity such as Melkart (Milk-qart, king of the city), related to Milcom of the Ammonites. Recently, on the strength of a late Carthaginian inscription, some scholars have claimed that 'Moloch' is not a name of a god at all, but of a particular type of sacrifice, and that it has been mistranslated: but this argument is not wholly convincing.

Discoveries in cemeteries in Carthage in 1921–25 (Fig. 19) and recently in her colonies (Sulcis, Tharros, Nora), show conclusively that it was the custom of the Carthaginian people, themselves colonists of the Phoenicians in the 8th–6th centuries B.C., to sacrifice babies by burning them on a pyre, and burying the ashes in an urn. Above it was placed a small stele, inscribed in Phoenician, usually with some such laconic formula, as 'X, son of Y, vowed this to Ba'al Hamman and to Tinit for hearing his voice'. These burials, placed close together, formed separate cemeteries which were called a 'Topheth'. Such a cemetery formerly existed outside Jerusalem in the Vale of Hinnom, and there is little reason to doubt this type of human sacrifice, probably of first-born, which was practised widely in Phoenicia and Canaan to placate the chief gods and ensure fertility of the land. Several such forms of sacrifices of male offspring were widespread among Western Semites, especially in time of calamity.

It was no doubt to wean the Hebrews from the temptations of these grim practices that the rite of 'redemption of the first-born' by payment of a monetary tax to the priests was instituted among the Jews.

The Carthaginians' custom of sacrificing their first-born children is well attested from Roman authors. The Romans, however, stamped out this native custom after their defeat of the Carthaginians in the Second Punic War.

Fig. 19—118333-118338.   Burial urns from the 'Topheth' of Salammbo, Carthage. *Syrian Room.*

And king Solomon made a navy of ships in Ezion-geber which is beside Eloth, on the shore of the Red Sea in the land of Edom, and Hiram sent in the navy his servants, shipmen that had knowledge of the sea, with the

FIG. 20—Phoenicians bringing monkeys; *Nimrud Gallery* 124562:
Height 2·36 m. × breadth 2·14 m.

servants of Solomon. And they came to Ophir, and fetched from thence gold, four hundred and twenty talents, and brought it to king Solomon. (I Kings ix. 26–8.)

IN about 950 B.C., Solomon succeeded his father, David, as king of a great Hebrew state, with its capital at Jerusalem. To carry out his ambitious plans, including the building of the magnificent temple and of the royal palace at Jerusalem, he sought the help of the neighbouring Phoenician ruler, Hiram (Ahiram), king of Tyre, which lay in what is now the modern state of Lebanon. Hiram provided skilled craftsmen and other workers, and precious raw materials, such as cedars of Lebanon and pinewood for building, and the two monarchs worked in close and fruitful harmony, regulated by a treaty (1 Kings v. 12), until the temple and palace were completed. One of the results of this Phoenician-Hebrew alliance was that the Hebrews were enabled to share in a maritime enterprise of the Phoenicians, the greatest sailors of their day, in return for giving them overland access to the more distant harbour facilities. The route in which the Phoenicians were most deeply interested was the access through the Gulf of Aqaba via the Red Sea to the Indian Ocean, which could not be at the mercy of Assyrian violence and jealousy. . . .

> 'Then went Solomon to Ezion-geber, and to Eloth, on the seashore in the land Edom. And Hiram sent him by the hands of his servants ships and servants that had knowledge of the sea; and they came with the servants of Solomon to Ophir, and fetched from thence four hundred and fifty talents of gold, and brought them to king Solomon.' (2 Chron. viii. 17.)

A port was duly established at the head of the gulf of Aqaba at Elath (where modern excavations by Dr. Nelson Glueck have revealed traces of copper-smelting), and the two kings were able to send an expedition every three years consisting of 'ships of Tarshish' (the name of a type of ocean-going Phoenician galley or man-of-war, with long prow for ramming). This fleet sailed to the land of Ophir, a mysterious district still unlocated but probably a part of India, perhaps the ancient port of Suppara, near Bombay. From here 'once every three years came the ships of Tarshish, bringing gold, silver, ivory, apes and peacocks' (1 Kings x. 22–24; 2 Chronicles ix. 10–11, 21–2). They also brought sandalwood. So the words in the Hebrew original for sandalwood, peacock and ape (Heb. *almug, algum, tukki* and *kôf*) are apparently of Indian origin (Tamil *agil, tokei,* and Sanskrit *kapi*) and the Indian location of Ophir seems more than likely.

The appearance of such Phoenician merchants—'servants of Hiram' —is well shown on a splendid Assyrian relief from the Palace of Ashurnasir-pal II (883–859 B.C.) at Nimrud. It shows two men, the former wearing a fully Phoenician dress, turban, long shirt and cloak thrown over the shoulder, with upturned boots, cracking his thumbs in sign of greeting to the king. Behind him is another wearing a Syrian coiffure with a bun of hair bound by a fillet, and a shorter shirt; he is holding two monkeys as royal gifts.

FIG. 21—A 'Ship of Tarshish': *Nineveh Gallery* 124772: Height 66 cm. × breadth 99 cm.

41

9. THE IVORY HOUSE OF AHAB

Now the rest of the acts of Ahab and all that he did and the ivory house which he built, and all the cities that he built, are they not written in the book of the Chronicles of the Kings of Israel? (1 Kings xxii. 39.)

THE ties of the northern Hebrew kingdom of Israel with the pagan Phoenician cities of the Lebanon, their immediate neighbours, were close, both culturally and politically, in the 9th century B.C. Ahab, King of Israel (about 850 B.C.), married a Phoenician princess from Tyre, Jezebel, and built a palace, decorated (or furnished) with ivory carvings of Phoenician type. Such buildings were considered by the psalmist (Ps. xiv. 8) as symbols of luxury, but by the prophet Amos, Ahab's contemporary, as tokens of evil living and oppression of the poor. 'And I will smite the winter-house with the summer-house; and the houses of ivory shall perish, and the great houses shall have an end, saith the Lord.' (Amos iii. 15.)

Excavations conducted at Sebaste, the site of Ahab's capital, Samaria, in 1931–5, by a joint Anglo-American expedition under Mr. J. W. Crowfoot, resulted in the discovery of finely carved ivory fragments, evidently from such a building. They included fragments of inlays of glass paste in ivory, representing floral motifs, and figured scenes in ivory, of a type now recognised as Phoenician work, similar pieces having been found at other sites. It is probable that they formed the decoration of furniture of the royal palace, though they were not found in its rooms, but dumped in rubbish pits near its enclosing wall. The finds were divided between the University Museum of Philadelphia, the Rockefeller Museum at Jerusalem (Jordan), and the Palestine Exploration Fund, London.

FIG. 22—L. 31–48.   Ivory fragments probably from Ahab's palace. (Lent by the
Palestine Exploration Fund.)

THE books of the Old Testament frequently refer to a type of heavenly being, or angel of God called *cherub* (plural *cherubim*). The term has passed into the English language untranslated. In the Bible it appears as a potent figure, symbolic of protection, a sort of sacred guardian of holy things. Two great cherubim, their wings outstretched, and touching at the wing tips, spanned the approach to the Holy of Holies in the temple built by Solomon, and others flanked figures of palm trees carved

FIG. 23—118163. Ivory panel carved with cherubim back to back. Phoenician work. Height 8·2 cms. Found in the North-West Palace, Nimrud (1845). *Syrian Room.*

in cedarwood there on the panelling (1 Kings vii. 23–29). A single figure in gold of a cherub still stood, nearly a thousand years later, in the second temple, the temple built by Herod. God himself was deemed to sit 'between the cherubim' (Exodus xxv. 2; 1 Samuel iv. 4), i.e. on a throne with cherubim as supporters.

There is little doubt that a *cherub* was the Hebrew name for the winged figure with lion's body and woman's head, which the Greeks called a sphinx. This composite figure, perhaps derived from Egypt, was at home in the Pantheon of the Phoenicians, to whom it probably represented the all-powerful goddess Ashtart, and was her sacred animal. From the Phoenicians it was taken over by the Hebrews, and divested of its heathen associations.

44

Cherubim or sphinxes are often illustrated in Phoenician art in heraldic groups, flanking palm trees or symbolic trees, especially in carved panels of ivory. The example illustrated here is from furniture made by Phoenician craftsmen and carried off as booty by the Assyrian kings to their capital, Kalhu (Nimrud), the Biblical Calah (Genesis x). This site was first excavated by A. H. Layard in 1845–7, and resulted in the finding of the first group of these ivories. Others have been found in the excavations of the British School of Archaeology in Iraq at the same site, re-opened by Sir Max Mallowan in 1951, and elsewhere. This and similar panels if greatly magnified illustrate what must have been the appearance of the symbolic figures within the temple of Solomon, c. 950 B.C.

11. SHALMANESER III (859–824 B.C.)

THE aggressive expansion of Assyria beyond her frontiers, begun by Ashurnasirpal II (883–859 B.C.) was continued by his son Shalmaneser III, a vigorous general; of his historical records, several editions survive. The earliest of these is on a monolith found in 1861 at Kurkh (ancient Tushkha) on the Tigris, about 20 miles south of Diyarbakr in southeastern Turkey. It shows on the front a representation of the king himself standing under the symbols of the gods, which he salutes. They are a moon (for the god Sin, god of the moon), lightning (for the weather god, Adad), horned cap (for Anu, god of the sky), star (for Ishtar, goddess of the morning and evening star), winged disc (for Ashur). The front and back of the monolith are covered with lines of writing in cuneiform script, which, after a poetic invocation of the gods and a hymn of praise of Shalmaneser, records in rhetorical language the events of his first six campaigns of conquests. Of these, the last is of present interest.

In his sixth year (853 B.C.), he records, he forded the Euphrates for the second time in flood, received the tribute of the Hittite kings of North Syria under the leadership of the king of Carchemish at Pitru (the Biblical Pethor, home of Balaam, Numbers xxii, 5, 22), and advanced southwards through Halman (Aleppo) against Irhuleni, king of Hamath (mod. Hama). This personage had organised a formidable coalition of 12 kings, with over 50,000 men, 3,900 chariots and 14,000 cavalry and 1,000 camels, to resist the Assyrians, including 20,000 soldiers from Hadad-ezer, king of Aram, and '2,000 chariots and 10,000 foot soldiers from Ahab, the Israelite [*Ahabbu* (mat) *Sir'ilaia*]' king of the northern Hebrew kingdom of Israel, and 10,000 soldiers of 'Ba'sa, son of Ruhubi [Rehob], King of Ammon'. The armies met in battle at Qarqar, near Hamath, on the Orontes, and the coalition was routed, with a loss of 14,000 men, or, according to later versions, 25,000, or even 29,000. In spite, however, of these great claims, the victory was not decisive, and three further Assyrian punitive campaigns against Aram and Hamath took place, without their succeeding, in fact, in finally defeating them. In Shalmaneser's eighteenth year, however (841–840 B.C.), Israel under Jehu, the successor of Ahab, submitted.

FIG. 24—118884.   Monolith of Shalmaneser III from Kurkh.
Height 2·20 m. *Assyrian Transept.*

47

AHAB, son of Omri, king of Israel, lost his life in battle in 850 B.C., fighting against the king of Damascus at Ramoth-gilead (1 Kings xxii. 29–36). He was succeeded by Jehu, a usurper, who broke the alliances with Phoenicia and Judah, and submitted to Assyria.

On an obelisk of black stone, discovered by A. H. Layard in 1846, Shalmaneser III, king of Assyria, depicted his triumphs over several kingdoms of Syria and the West. In the second row from the top is a figure dressed in the costume of the western Semites (see below), who pays homage by bowing to the ground, while his servants bring gifts. He seems to depict Jehu, who in the text is called 'son of Omri'. The

FIG. 25.

Assyrians in this period used the term 'House of Omri' to cover both the Kingdom of Israel, governed from Omri's capital, Samaria, and for the family of Omri, in which they apparently included Jehu.

Above the scene is written in Assyrian cuneiform, '*The tribute of Jehu, son of Omri, I received from him silver, gold, a golden bowl, a golden vase with pointed bottom, golden tumblers, golden buckets, tin, a staff for a king* [and] purukhti *fruits.*' This event appears to have taken place in 841 B.C.

This is the earliest picture of an Israelite which has survived. It shows the Israelite king wearing the western Semitic dress (common also to the Phoenicians)—a low turban and long over-garment.

48

FIG. 26—118885. The 'Jehu Stele' or 'Black Obelisk'.
Black stone. Height 1·98 m. *Assyrian Transept.*

In 745 B.C., after a period of decline and disorder, a soldier-prince named Pulu, or Pul, as recorded both in the Bible (2 Kings xv. 19), and in Babylonian tradition, ascended the throne of Assyria and was crowned under the name of Tukulti-apal-Esharra. He is to us more generally known as Tiglath-pileser III (745–727 B.C.), the form in which this name appears in the Bible.

A vigorous leader, he reorganised the army and state and carried the Assyrian arms far and wide. In 734 B.C. he sent an army against Phoenicia, Hamath and Israel, under the generalship of the officer called the *rab shaqu*, chief cup-bearer, in Hebrew called Rabshakeh (2 Kings xvii. 17 ff.). The Phoenician kings of Tyre and Byblos submitted, followed by Rezin of Damascus, the Aramaean, and Menahem of Israel, who sent tribute 'in order to receive the kingship in his hands' (2 Kings xv. 19). Between 743 and 738 B.C., Pekah revolted against Menahem, and the Assyrian forces returned, invading Moab, Gilead and Galilee, parts of which Tiglath-pileser claimed to have annexed. To this episode, we may refer a relief from Tiglath-pileser's palace showing the surrender of the city of Astartu (i.e. Ashtoreth-Karnaim in Gilead), clearly labelled in cuneiform script.

The city, standing on a mound, is surrounded by a double wall with towers, and has a citadel at one end. Assyrian officers are driving out booty in the form of fat-tailed rams, and Hebrew prisoners are carrying bundles, wearing west Semitic dress, turban with floppy top, fringed mantle and shirt and boots with upward-curving toes.

In the central band is a passage from Tiglath-pileser III's historical *Annals*, describing his campaigns in the north of Assyria.

In the panel below is the king himself, standing in his state chariot beneath a parasol, and saluting some persons, perhaps officers with prisoners, which were probably on an adjacent slab, now lost.

FIG. 27—118908. The Capture of Astartu. Relief. From the South-West
Palace, Nimrud. Limestone. Height 1·88 m. × length 1·95 m.

In the twelfth year of Ahaz, king of Judah, began Hoshea, the son of Elah, to reign in Samaria over Israel (and reigned) *nine years. And he did that which was evil in the sight of the Lord, yet not as the kings of Israel that went before him. Against him came Shalmaneser, king of Assyria; and Hoshea became his servant and brought him presents. And the king of Assyria found conspiracy in Hoshea: for he had sent messengers to So, king of Egypt and offered no present to the king of Assyria, as he had done year by year. Therefore the king of Assyria shut him up and bound him in prison. Then the king of Assyria came up throughout all the land and went up to Samaria and besieged it three years. In the ninth year of Hoshea, the king of Assyria took Samaria and carried Israel away unto Assyria and placed them in Halah and in Habor on the river of Gozan and in the cities of the Medes.* (2 Kings xvii. 3 ff.)

THE Assyrian king, Shalmaneser V (727–722 B.C.) the son and successor of Tiglath-pileser III, continued his father's policy of pressure against the western cities of Phoenicia and Palestine and according to the Assyrian eponym list, the main campaigns of 725–723 B.C. were directed against the powerful city of Samaria. In the next year Shalmaneser died (723/2) but the city apparently fell to him. His successor, Sargon, claims in his annals to have captured the city of Samaria and appointed a governor of his own.

> I surrounded and deported as prisoners 27,290 of its inhabitants, together with their chariots . . . and the gods in whom they trusted. From them I equipped 200 chariots for my army units, while the rest I made to take up their lot within Assyria. I restored the city of Samaria and made it more habitable than before. I brought into it people from the countries conquered by my own hands. My official I set over them as district governor and reckoned them as people of Assyria itself. (Nimrud Prism IV. 25–41.)

A relief from the south-east façade of Sargon's palace at Khorsabad, which he built to commemorate his victories, shows the king in life size, wearing his regalia, receiving his vizier.

The Israelites of Samaria were deported, as we are told by the Bible, to Halah and Habor and Media. Halah is unidentified, but Habor is the city Guzana, on the river Habur, in north Syria, which was conquered by Adad-Nirari III and made into an Assyrian province in 794 B.C. It possessed a palace built in the 10th century B.C. by one of its Aramaean

Fig. 28—B.M. 118822. Relief from the Palace of Sargon at Khorsabad, showing the king receiving his minister or other high officer, possibly the turtanu (commander-in-chief). Height 2·98 m. *Assyrian Entrance.*

rulers, Kapara, which was excavated in 1911–13 and 1927–9 by Baron Max von Oppenheim. Some sculptures from its walls may be seen in the Syrian Room.

The inhabitants of other captured cities which Sargon imported into Samaria to repopulate it were regarded as heathens in the eyes of the Jews after their return from captivity, and there was lasting hostility towards them, which is reflected in the parable of Jesus of the good, if exceptional, Samaritan. But the Samaritans, who accept the authority of the Pentateuch but not the Prophets or Talmud, lived on, preserving their own customs and scriptures and even their own version of the Old Phoenician Alphabet to this day. An example of their script is preserved on a 13th century A.D. inscription on stone (Fig. 29). It bears extracts from the Pentateuch (Deuteronomy vi. 4; xxiii. 15; xxviii. 6) and probably stood in a doorway of a building, like a Hebrew 'mezuza', or doorpost inscription.

FIG. 29—B.M. 127387.   Samaritan inscription, on limestone block.
41·1 cm. × 31·8 cm. × 16·5 cm.

15. SENNACHERIB AND HEZEKIAH

Now in the fourteenth year of Hezekiah did Sennacherib, king of Assyria, come up against all the fenced cities of Judah and took them (2 Kings xviii. 13.)

Pursuing the career of militaristic expansion of his predecessor, the Assyrian king Sennacherib (705–681 B.C.) directed his first campaign against the Chaldaean king of Babylon, Merodach-baladan, and routed him. In his third year he turned westwards against Phoenicia and Palestine. Taking up the excuse that Hezekiah, king of Judah, had imprisoned a friend of Assyria, the Philistine chieftain Padi, ruler of Ekron, Sennacherib's army marched past Jerusalem to the Egyptian border where it repulsed an Egyptian attack in a battle at Eltekeh. But the city of Lachish, remaining faithful to the king of Judah, refused to admit him and he was compelled to take it by siege (see below, The Siege of Lachish). This event is not explicitly described in Sennacherib's royal annals, but is implied in Isaiah xxxvi–xxxvii, 36–39 and in 2 Kings xviii where the text goes on to say:

> and Hezekiah, king of Judah, sent to the king of Assyria to Lachish saying, I have offended; return from me; that which thou puttest on me will I bear. And the king of Assyria appointed to Hezekiah, king of Judah, three hundred talents of silver and thirty talents of gold . . . and the king of Assyria sent Tartan and Rabsaris and Rabshakeh from Lachish to King Hezekiah with a great host against Jerusalem.

While the Biblical account describes how the invading army retreated in the face of a plague, a six-sided clay prism, often called after its first owner the 'Taylor Prism', found at Nineveh, inscribed in cuneiform script in 691 B.C. with the final edition of Sennacherib's annals, describes these events slightly differently:

> As for Hezekiah the Jew, who did not submit to my yoke, 46 of his strong, walled cities, as well as the small cities in their neighbourhood, which were without number,—by escalade[1] and by bringing up siege engines (?), by attacking and storming on foot, by mines, tunnels and breaches (?), I besieged and took [those cities]. 200,150 people, great and small, male and female, horses, mules asses, camels, cattle and sheep, without number, I brought away from them and counted as spoil. Himself, like a caged bird, I shut up in Jerusalem, his royal city. Earthworks I threw up against him,— the one coming out of his city gate I turned back to his misery. The cities

---

[1] *Lit.*, by causing (them) to tread the ramp or incline.

FIG. 30—B.M. 91032. Clay prism containing the final edition of Sennacherib's
Annals, dated to 691 B.C. Height 38·5 cm. × width 15 cm. *Room of Writing*.

of his, which I had despoiled, I cut off from his land and to Mitinti, king of Ashdod, Padi, king of Ekron, and Silli-bel, king of Gaza, I gave them. And [thus] I diminished his land. I added to the former tribute, and laid upon him [v., them] as their yearly payment, a tax [in the form of] gifts for my majesty. As for Hezekiah, the terrifying splendour of my majesty overcame him, and the Urbi [Arabs] and his mercenary [?] troops which he had brought in to strengthen Jerusalem, his royal city, deserted him [*lit.*, took leave]. In addition to 30 talents of gold and 800 talents of silver, (there were) gems, antimony, jewels [?], large sandu-stones, couches of ivory, house chairs of ivory, elephant's hide, ivory, [*lit.*, elephant's "teeth'], maple (?), boxwood, all kinds of valuable [heavy] treasures, as well as his daughters, his harem, his male and female musicians, [which] he had [them] bring after me to Nineveh, my royal city. To pay tribute and to accept [*lit.*, do] servitude he despatched his messengers.

A clay tablet (K1295) excavated at Nineveh in the palace of Sennacherib describes some of the tribute of the kingdom of Judah, sent to Nineveh with that of neighbouring kingdoms:

FIG. 31.—K. 1295.   Clay tablet.
Size: height 4·4 cm × width 3·6 cm.

'Two minas of gold from the inhabitants of Bit-Ammon (*mat Bit-Amman-na-a-a*); one mina of gold from the inhabitants of Moab (*mat Mu-'-ba-a-a*); ten minas of silver from the inhabitants of Judah (*mat Ia-u-da-a-a*); [. . . mi]nas of silver from the inhabitants of [Edom] (*mat [U-du-ma]-a-a*) . . .

[reverse]
. . . the inhabitants of Byblos, the district officers of the king, my lord, have brought.'

This tablet appears to belong to the reign of Sennacherib (i.e. 705–681 B.C.).

58

FIG. 32—B.M. 124901. Relief from the Palace of Sennacherib at Kuyunjik, showing men of Lachish in the Assyrian Royal Guard. Limestone. Height 1·60 m. × width 1·09 m. *Assyrian Basement.*

16. THE SIEGE OF LACHISH

FROM the implied reference in the Book of Kings (see above) to the delays which kept Sennacherib at Lachish, one could infer that that city was holding out against a siege by the Assyrians, and then fell in 700 B.C. This was first confirmed by the discovery by Layard in 1849 of reliefs in the palace of Sennacherib at Nineveh, in Room XXXVI. These reliefs enable us to reconstruct the events of the siege, which they illustrate in some detail (Figs. 33–4). It is, in fact, duly identified by a cuneiform caption: 'Sennacherib, king of the universe, king of Assyria sat upon a throne, while the booty of Lachish passed before him.' The city stands on stony ground, depicted by a scale pattern amid olive groves and vineyards. A great siege-mound, its surface covered with logs, has been thrown by the Assyrians against the city wall and gate. Under cover of a protecting fire of arrows, shot by archers advancing behind their shields, the siege machines, resembling modern tanks, climb up the mound to use their battering rams. This mound was not so steep; nor was it built in strips arranged in a V-shaped pattern as it is shown. This is the result of the artist's unsuccessful attempt at rendering a single sloping mound, in ignorance of the laws of perspective. From the gate, the inhabitants stream out in surrender, taking their possessions with them; some prisoners, stripped naked, have been brutally impaled on stakes. Others, wearing long garments and bareheaded, showing curly hair, are led before the king, who sits wearing his royal dress, on his royal throne before his tent, his chariot standing by. These prisoners are singled out for his particular displeasure and are either beheaded or flayed alive. These are probably Hezekiah's men, the Hebrews who influenced the city to resist, and are probably the earliest representations of Judaeans, since the only other representation of a Hebrew, that on the 'Black Obelisk' (see above, Fig. 26) shows Jehu or his emissary wearing Phoenician dress, he being not a Judaean (of the south of Palestine) but an Israelite of the North, from the kingdom of Israel, the frontiers of which marched with those of Phoenicians.

The other prisoners who are spared, carrying out their possessions on bullock carts (or in one case, on a camel) under guard, wear a different dress—a kilt, and a headdress consisting of a scarf, the end hanging down by the ear. From an account of his reign, written after his fifth campaign, we learn what became of these persons, and Sennacherib describes how he carried off the various peoples whom he had defeated to help build the palace at Kuyunjik which the reliefs ornamented: 'The people of Chaldea, the Aramaeans, the Mannaeans, the people of the land of Kue

F IG. 33—124910–12. The Surrender of Lachish. Reliefs from the Palace of Sennacherib. Height 2·57 m. *Assyrian Saloon.*

61

and Khilakku [= Cilicia], of Philistia and Tyre, who had not submitted to my yoke, I deported [from their lands] and made them carry the headpad and mould bricks.' Scenes of this activity are to be seen on reliefs in the Nineveh Gallery. The people of Lachish were evidently reckoned by the Assyrians as among the Philistines, and a sculpture showing men of Lachish taking part in the building of Sennacherib's palace was found in 1848. Some of the more reliable Lachishites, however, seem to have been enlisted as a special contingent into the Assyrian army, since we find them in another relief from the palace as members of the royal guard, escorting a religious procession to the Temple of Ishtar (Fig. 32).

After Sennacherib's death, a revolt took place in Assyria, and his palace was burnt. Traces of burning can be seen at the bottom of the relief Fig. 33.

In 1934 excavations were opened at the site of Lachish (Tell Duweir) by the Wellcome Archaeological Expedition, supported by the late Sir Charles Marston, under the leadership of J. L. Starkey. Unfortunately, Starkey was murdered by Arab marauders in 1938 and the excavation ceased; but he had been able to complete the excavation of the city walls and city gateway of the Iron Age. In this gateway in Level III, in which the fortifications were cut down, were found actual objects from the Assyrian assault, iron arrowheads, some too of bone, made by the defenders when supplies ran short, fragments of scale armour, sling stones, and a helmet-crest of bronze, belonging to some Assyrian, and olive stones, suggesting that the battle was fought in the autumn.

FIG. 34—124907–9.   The booty of Lachish. Reliefs from the Palace of Sennacherib. Limestone. Height 2·57 m. *Assyrian Saloon.*

Fig. 35—Olive stones and sling-stones from the Siege of Lachish. Presented by the Wellcome Historical Foundation.

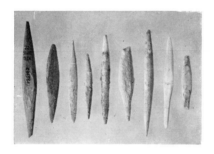

Fig. 36—Bronze, bone and iron arrow-heads from the Siege of Lachish.
Presented by the Wellcome Historical Foundation.

17. THE TOMB OF SHEBNA, A ROYAL STEWARD

Thus saith the Lord God of hosts, Go, get thee unto this Treasurer, even unto Shebna, which is over the house and say: What hast thou here? and whom hast thou here, that thou hast hewed thee out a sepulchre here, as he that heweth him out a sepulchre on high, and that graveth an habitation, for himself in a rock?

Isaiah. xxii. 15, 16.

An important discovery was made in 1870 by the famous French archaeologist, Charles Clermont-Ganneau, in Silwan (the ancient Siloam), an Arab village outside Jerusalem, on the eastern side of the Kedron Valley. Here there is a rock-cut chamber tomb entered through a door and, above the door, the present inscription in archaic Hebrew (Phoenician) letters was incised in a sunken panel.

The text has been badly defaced, and defied interpretation until it was brilliantly deciphered in 1953 by an Israeli scholar, Professor N. Avigad, as follows:

1. '*This is* [the sepulchre of . . .]-*yahu, who is Over the House* (i.e., a Royal Steward). *There is no silver and no gold here*
2. *but* [his bones] *and the bones of his slave-wife with him. Cursed be the man who*
3. *will open this.*'

It seems almost certain that the mutilated name is to be completed as Sheban-yahu (this name could be abbreviated to Shebna). Shebna was a Royal Steward of Hezekiah, king of Judah, and was rebuked by the prophet Isaiah for having built himself a too conspicuous tomb in his lifetime (Isaiah xxii. 15, 16).

This text, despite its condition, is a fine specimen of Hebrew monumental writing of the period of the Kings. It is also the third longest monumental inscription in Hebrew and the first known text of a Hebrew sepulchral inscription from the pre-Exilic period.

Fig. 37—125205. Epitaph of a Royal Steward. Limestone: length, 1.32 m. Early 7th century B.C. *Room of Writing.* (The letters on the original have been painted with white for clarity.)

IN 1934, the Wellcome Archaeological Research Expedition to the Near East undertook its third season of work at the site of Tell-el-Duweir, since then identified with the Biblical site of Lachish, a fortress city on the frontier of Palestine and Egypt. (See above, No. 16.) In the following spring, the excavators found in the ruins of a room in part of the gate-

FIG. 38—125701. Letter written with a pen and ink on potsherd.
Size: 10 × 8 cm. *Room of Writing.*

way to the city, eighteen 'ostraca', i.e., broken potsherds which were commonly used for writing on in antiquity in the absence of papyrus or other suitable material. Three more were found in 1938. (Some of these ostraca are now in the Rockefeller Museum, Jerusalem.)

Though the writing on many of these ostraca is too faint to be now read, it appears from those which are legible that they were letters received by Ya'osh, the military governor of Lachish, from Hosha'yahu, a subordinate officer in charge of a nearby town during the invasion of Palestine by the Babylonians which ended in the siege and destruction of Jerusalem in 587 B.C. (See below, No. 19.)

Of these, Letter I (125701) is a list of Hebrew names: Gemaryahu, son of Hissilyahu, Yaazanyahu, son of Tobshillem, Hagab, son of Yaazanyahu, Mibtahyahu, son of Yirmeyahu, Mattanyahu, son of Neriyahu.

FIG. 39—125702. Letter, written with pen and ink on potsherd.
Size: 9 × 10 cm. *Room of Writing.*

Though several of these names occur in the Old Testament, especially in the Book of Jeremiah (for Gemaryahu, cf. Gemariah, Jer. xxxv. 3, x. 8, xii. 1 : for Mattanyahu, cf. Mattaniah, 2 Kings xxiv. 17: for Neriyahu, Neriah, Jer. xxxii, 12, xxxvi, 14, 32; i. 59), they cannot be proved to be connected with these persons.

The remaining letters, some of which are only partially legible, deal with military matters. Letter II (125702) mentions the name of God (YHWH) at the beginning (right-hand end) of line 2.

19. THE END OF ASSYRIA, THE FALL OF NINEVEH, AND THE CAPTURE OF JERUSALEM

THE decline and fall of the mighty Assyrian empire which had lorded it over the entire Near East was described by the Hebrew prophet Nahum. Of this event there are contemporary Babylonian accounts. The Babylonians themselves, subjugated by the Assyrians, kept careful historical records, and the British Museum possesses several parts of a cuneiform Babylonian chronicle (B.M. 25127, 21901, 22047, 21946, 25124 and 35382), which tell the history of those stirring events. In 626 B.C., Babylonia (in these records using the ancient name of Akkad) took the lead among the subject powers of Assyria in attempting to regain her independence and throw off the Assyrian yoke. In 615 B.C., the Medes, by then settled in NW. Iran, led by Kashtaritu (called by the Greeks Kyaxares), moved against the Assyrians and entered the province of Arraphu (Kirkuk); in 614, they captured the city Assur, and formed an alliance with the Babylonians. In the month of Ab (= August) 612 B.C., the city of Nineveh fell to their combined assault, with the aid of another ally called the 'Umman-manda', probably Scythians, perhaps Medes.

'[In the fourteenth year] the king of Akkad called out his army [and marched to . . . .] the king of the Umman-manda with the king of Akkad [. . . . .] they met each other
The king of Akkad [. . . . . Kyaxa]res [. . . . .] he made to cross and they marched along the bank of the river Tigris and [. . . . .] against Nineveh [. . . . .] they encamped (?)
From the month of Sivan to the month of Ab three UŠ-[measures . . . . . . they advanced ?]
A strong attack they made against the city, and in the month of Ab, [the . . . .th day the city was captured . . . .] a great defeat of the chief [people] was made.
On that day Sin-šar-iškun, the Assyrian king [. . . . . . .]
The great spoil of the city and temple they carried off and [turned] the city into a ruin-mound and heaps of debri[s . . . .]

The Babylonians, under their king Nabopolassar, followed up their successes by pursuing the defeated Assyrians into North Syria, who took refuge in Harran, west of the Euphrates. But Pharaoh Necho sent to the aid of the sinking Assyrian kingdom an Egyptian army which marched to the Euphrates in 605 B.C. A clash took place at Carchemish, the great city commanding the ford of the Euphrates. This battle is described by Josephus, *Antiquities*, x. 6, and referred to in 2 Kings xxiii. 29, and 2, Chronicles xxv. 20. The Babylonian army, led by Nebuchadnezzar, son of Nabopolassar, was victorious. Arrowheads

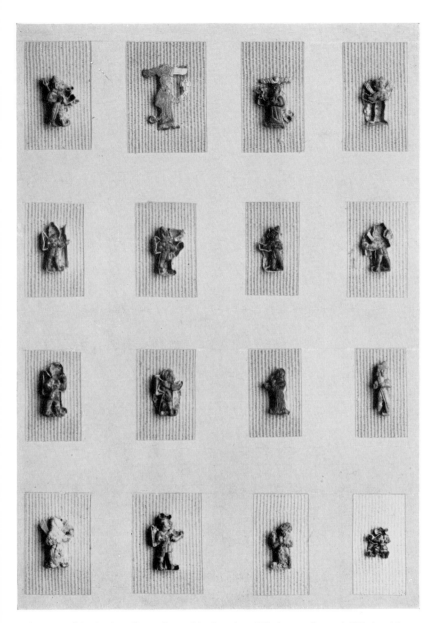

Figures of lapis lazuli set in gold showing Hittite gods and Hittite kings.
From a royal robe, Carchemish. (see fig. 45). *Hittite Room.*

FIG. 40.

(Fig. 42) and objects including the shield of an Ionian Greek soldier (Fig. 41) from the battle in the suburbs of Carchemish were found in the excavations conducted there in 1911 by the British Museum. In the battle, the last titular priest-king of Carchemish seems to have fallen,

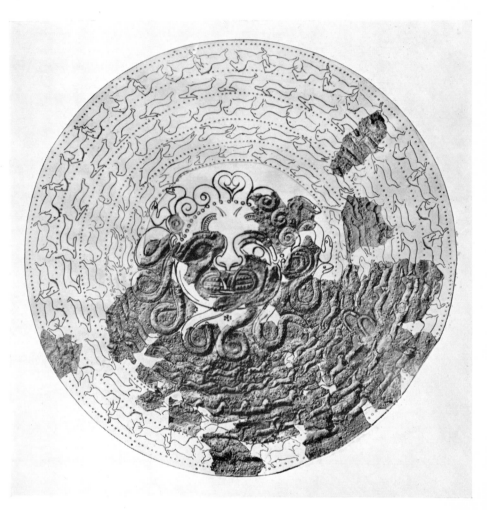

FIG. 41—B.M. 116253. Bronze repoussé covering of a shield of East Greek type from House D, Carchemish, showing Gorgon's head and running animals. *Syrian Room.*

for a funerary urn was found buried in a room in the North West Fort containing a cremation burial and what was evidently a Hittite royal robe of gold thread, then already some hundreds of years old, ornamented with tiny lapis lazuli figures of Hittite gods set in gold cloisons greeting a Hittite king in the style of the Hittite Empire (Figs. 40, 45).

The Babylonians, having now command of Syria, followed up their advantage and marched toward Egypt in 601, but were repulsed.

In 599 B.C., Nebuchadnezzar, in his seventh year, opened a fresh series of campaigns, and since Jehoiakim, king of Jerusalem, had failed to pay his tribute to his new master, Nebuchadnezzar turned against Judah. The Chronicle, recently published for the first time, gives the exact date of the fall of Jerusalem, commemorated in the Bible (2 Kings

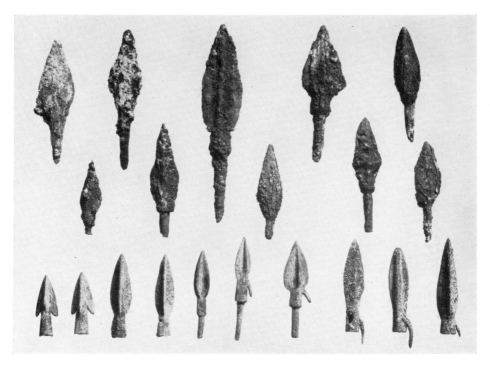

FIG. 42—B.M. 116196–116220. Bronze and iron arrowheads from House D, Carchemish.

xxiv. 10–17) and traditionally held to have occurred on the 9th Ab. In fact it fell on 2nd Adar, i.e., 15th/16th March, 597 B.C., as recorded by the Babylonian Chronicle (Fig. 44):

'In the seventh year, the month of Kislev, the king of Akkad mustered his troops, marched to the Hatti-land, and encamped against (i.e., besieged) the city of Judah and on the second day of the month of Adar he seized the city and captured the king. He appointed there a king of his own choice (*lit.*: heart), received its heavy tribute and sent (them) to Babylon.'

73

Jehoiakim died shortly before the fall of the city, and was succeeded by Jehoiachin, who was carried off to captivity. He was replaced by the king of Nebuchadnezzar's choice, a Babylonian protegé, Mattaniah, the youthful uncle of Jehoiakim, who changed his name to Zedekiah (2

Fig. 43—B.M. 21901.   Clay tablet inscribed with part of
Babylonian chronicle, years 616–609 B.C. *Room of Writing.*

Kings xxiv. 17; Jeremiah xxxvii. 1). Jehoiachin and his family languished in prison in Babylon and died there. A recently-published text in cuneiform preserved in Berlin, records the issue of rations to him and his family in prison.

Fig. 44—B.M. 21946. Clay tablet recording battle of Carchemish and Fall of Jerusalem. *Room of Writing*.

Fig. 45—Detail of figures in Fig. 40. *Hittite Room*.

20. THE ACCESSION OF CYRUS THE MEDE

Now in the first year of Cyrus king of Persia, that the word of the Lord by the mouth of Jeremiah might be accomplished, the Lord stirred up the spirit of Cyrus king of Persia, that he made a proclamation throughout all his kingdom, and put it also in writing saying:

Thus saith Cyrus king of Persia: All the kingdoms of the earth hath the Lord, the God of heaven, given me; and he hath charged me to build him an house in Jerusalem which is in Judah. Whosoever there is among you of all his people, his God be with him, and let him go up to Jerusalem, which is in Judah, and build the house of the Lord the god of Israel (he is God) which is in Jerusalem.

EZRA i. 1–3

FIG. 46—90920. Clay cylinder inscribed in cuneiform with text of Cyrus the Great, king of Persia. Length 23 cm. *Persian Landing.*

IN 539 B.C., Kuraš or Cyrus the Mede, the descendant of Teispes, king of Anshan, suddenly marched against Nabunaid, or Nabonidus, king of Babylon, and overthrew the empire of the Chaldean dynasty, which had reigned in Babylon since the fall of Nineveh in 612 B.C. (see above, No. 19) and the collapse of the world empire of the Assyrians. Entering the Chaldaean's capital, Babylon, without a battle, Cyrus became heir to the Babylonian empire and united it with that of the Medes. The event is described with some confusions in the Book of Daniel iv–v. In this clay barrel-shaped document, which must have formed part of the foundation deposit of some building, Cyrus describes how Marduk, the god of Babylon, turned with disgust away from Nabonidus on account of his impieties and his injustices, and appointed Cyrus to replace him.

Upon their (the Babylonians) complaints the lord of the gods became terribly angry and [he departed from] their region, (also) the (other) gods living among them left their mansions, wroth that he had brought (them) into Babylon (Su.an.na^{ki}). (But) Marduk [who does care for] . . . on account of (the fact that) the sanctuaries of all their settlements were in ruins and the inhabitants of Sumer and Akkad had become like (living) dead, turned back (his countenance) [his] an[ger] [abated] and he had mercy (upon them). He scanned and looked (through) all the countries, searching for a righteous ruler willing to lead him (i.e., Marduk) (in the annual procession). (Then) he pronounced the name of Cyrus (Ku-ra-aš), king of Anshan, declared him (*lit.*: pronounced [his] name) to be(come) the ruler of all the world.

Without any battle, he (Marduk) made him enter his town, Babylon, sparing Babylon any calamity. He delivered into his (i.e., Cyrus') hands Nabonidus, the king who did not worship him (i.e., Marduk). All the inhabitants of Babylon, as well as of the entire country of Sumer and Akkad, princes and governors bowed to him (Cyrus) and kissed his feet, jubilant that he had received the kingship, and with shining faces. Happily they greeted him as a master, through whose help they had come (again) to life from death (and) that all had been spared damage and disaster, and they worshipped his name.

In the concluding section, Cyrus describes his new religious policy of toleration, reversing the Babylonian policy of carrying captive both foreign peoples and their gods:

[As to the region] from [. . . . .] as far as Ashur and Susa, Agade, Eshnunna, the towns Zamban, Me-Turnu, Der, as well as the region of the Gutians, I returned to these sacred cities on the other side of the Tigris, the sanctuaries of which have been ruins for a long time, the images which used to live therein and established for them permanent sanctuaries. I (also) gathered all their (former) inhabitants and returned (to them) their habitations.

From the opening of the Book of Ezra (i. 1–3) we know of the momentous application of this enactment to the captive Jews, who were thereby allowed to return home and rebuild the Temple at Jerusalem. The wording of this quotation recalls, in a general way, the beginning of the text of the Cyrus cylinder which we have quoted above.

21. DARIUS, THE GREAT KING, AND THE PALACE OF SHUSHAN

THE world empire established by Cyrus the Mede after his overthrow of the Babylonians did not long remain in the control of the Medes. After the death of Cyrus' son, Cambyses, in 522 B.C., and a civil war that rent the Eastern world, Darius, son of Hystaspes, a Persian prince, made himself the master of the conjoint empire of the Medes and Persians which was to last for nearly 200 years. This empire had two capitals, the one at Ekbatana (modern Hamadan) and the other at Susa ('Shushan the Palace', of the Book of Esther). It is clear that Darius, whose reign is referred to by the prophets Haggai and Zachariah, continued the tolerant policy of Cyrus in matters of religion, as the Book of Daniel, chapter vi, implies.

FIG. 47—89132.   Seal—Agate. Height 3·7 cm. × diameter 1·6 cm.
Persian landing

In Susa Darius built a palace in about 490 B.C., extensive remains of which have been found by the French excavators. It was decorated with friezes of coloured tiles, showing divine animals and floral patterns. In particular, a handsome frieze of gaily coloured tiles in relief representing in life-size a parade of the Great King's bodyguard of Bowmen, called the Immortals, may be mentioned. A figure from this frieze is in this Museum, the rest being in the Louvre. It shows a bowman wearing long Elamite dress, holding a spear.

Another important document illustrating the reign of Darius is his official cylinder seal, discovered in Egypt, which, under his son, became part of the Persian empire. Such seals were used from time immemorial in Mesopotamia, usually for rolling an impression on to clay tablets inscribed in cuneiform script. This seal, very finely cut, shows the king hunting a lion from a chariot. It is inscribed with his name and title, 'Darius the Great King' in three official languages of the Persian empire: Old Persian, Elamite and Babylonian cuneiform. Some scholars, however, believe that this seal is not that of Darius the Great (521–486 B.C.), but of a later successor, Darius II (423–405 B.C.).

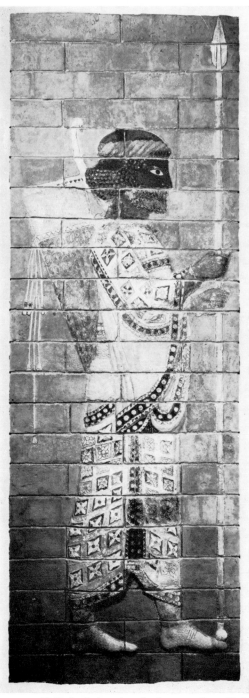

FIG. 48—132525. Relief of glazed polychrome tiles. Height 1·47 m.
Lent by the Musée du Louvre. *Persian Landing*.

22. THE DEAD SEA SCROLLS

IN 1947, an Arab goatherd, chasing a goat near the Dead Sea among the cliffs near a ruin known as Khirbet Qumran, found a cave containing ancient Hebrew manuscripts which had been originally stored in cylindrical jars. These manuscripts were the now famous 'Dead Sea Scrolls', which are generally believed to be the library of a monastery at Qumran of Essenes—a sect of extremely religious Jews who withdrew themselves here from the world of unrighteousness to dwell and study the sacred writings in the wilderness. To judge from remains of scrolls, often fragmentary, from several caves, their library appears to have included all the books of the Old Testament and the *Apocrypha* except *Esther*. In addition, they possessed some sectarian works. These finds of texts, far older and more extensive than any till then known, have thrown an entirely new light on Biblical studies, and the excavations in and around Qumran have brought all manner of new information about this sect and its beliefs and practices. It appears that their monastery at Khirbet Qumran was destroyed by the Roman armies at the same time as Jerusalem, in the Jewish Revolt of A.D. 66–70, in anticipation of which the sectaries hid their precious library in the secret fastnesses of the cliffs. The settlement is dated to the 1st century B.C. and 1st century A.D. by finds of coins and the pottery it contained. As it also included jars of this cylindrical type, there is good reason to suggest that the Dead Sea Scrolls which those jars contained in the caves were written in the settlement itself, and the actual writing room has been tentatively identified.

FIG. 49—131444A. Linen cloth wrapper for Scroll, 33·6 × 26·7 cm.

FIG. 50—131444. Clay pot, undecorated, with lid. Restored. Height 56 cm.

23. REMINISCENCES OF THE TEMPLE OF HEROD:
THE OSSUARY OF NICANOR

DURING the period of the 1st century B.C. and most of the 1st century A.D., in the lifetime of Christ, many Jews of Jerusalem practised the custom of burying their dead first in the soil, and then, after disintegration of the body, removing the bones and preserving them in a

FIG. 51—Greek and Hebrew inscriptions on Ossuary of Nicanor.

stone chest, or ossuary, of limestone which they placed in a burial chamber. This practice probably ceased when Jerusalem was destroyed by the Romans in A.D. 70. Many such ossuaries have been found in the vicinity of Jerusalem. They are usually rather simply decorated with floral or geometrical designs, which may perhaps possess a symbolic meaning. Sometimes they are briefly inscribed in Greek or Hebrew. One in the British Museum is of especial interest, since it bears on the

Fig. 52—126392. Limestone ossuary. Found in 1870, and presented to the Palestine Exploration Fund, London, by Mr. Hay, Acting U.S. Consul in Jerusalem; transferred to the British Museum 1903. Height 43 cm.

Fig. 53—126395. Limestone Ossuary of Nicanor, with traces of red paint. Height 38 cm. Found in a catacomb in grounds of Mr. J. Gray-Hill, on the Mount of Olives, 1903, by whom it was presented to the Palestine Exploration Fund.

short side the words in Greek 'ὀστᾶ τῶν τοῦ Νεικάνορος Ἀλεξανδρέως ποιήσαντος τὰς θύρας' 'Bones of the family of Nicanor the Alexandrian, who made the doors', and in Hebrew merely 'Nicanor Alexa'. This refers to Nicanor, a wealthy Jew of Alexandria (where there was a great Jewish community). This person presented a pair of great gates of bronze or Corinthian brass to the Temple of Herod. They were 10 cubits wide, with a chamber either side. It was one of the seven gates giving access to the Inner Court, but was the only one on the East side; furthermore, while the others were all of gold, the Nicanor gate alone was of bronze, and in view of its fame, it would appear that it was of great beauty, sufficient to face comparison with the others. The Nicanor gate stood at the head of a flight of 15 steps from the Court of the Women. According to the Talmud, it was believed that though the other gates were altered to gold, those of Nicanor remained of bronze, their special sanctity having been shown in the following way. While Nicanor was bringing them by sea to Joppa, a gale blew up, and they were in imminent danger of sinking; but, by a miracle, they were saved.

The second ossuary (126392) was found in 1870 in a 'cave', i.e., presumably a chamber tomb, in the Valley of the Convent of the Cross and contained then only a clay lamp, now lost. On the front side it has a design of rosettes about a central column, framed in sprays of leaves, perhaps of myrtle (Fig. 52). Its lid is decorated with an arcade of eight arches, resting on columns with capitals of roughly Corinthian type (Fig. 54). This is one of the earliest representations of the arcade in ancient art, earlier than any actual surviving example, the arcade being a form of architecture of which the earliest actually surviving example is found at Leptis Magna, dated to about A.D. 100. It seems very likely that this ossuary decoration imitates some well-known building and, if so, this is most likely to have been the Temple of Herod, completed in A.D. 64.

FIG. 54.

BIBLIOGRAPHY

1. THE BABYLONIAN LEGEND OF THE FLOOD

E. W. Budge, *The Rise and Progress of Assyriology* (London, 1925), pp. 112–114, 152–3.

G. Smith, *Assyrian Discoveries* (London, 1875); *The Chaldean Account of Genesis* (London, 1876).

J. V. Kinnier-Wilson, 'The Story of the Flood' in D. Winton Thomas (ed.) *Documents from Old Testament Times* [abbreviated as *DOTT*] (London, 1958), pp. 17–26.

E. A. Speiser, 'Akkadian Myths and Epics' in J. B. Pritchard (ed.), *Ancient Near Eastern Texts Relating to the Old Testament* [abbreviated as *ANET*] (Princeton, 1950), pp. 93–97.

E. Sollberger, *The Babylonian Legend of the Flood* (British Museum; London, 1962).

M. E. L. Mallowan, 'Noah's Flood Reconsidered' *Iraq*, xxvi (1964), pp. 62–83.

2. THE 'AMARNA LETTERS' AND THE CITIES OF CANAAN

C. Bezold and E. A. W. Budge, *The Tell-el-Amarna Tablets in the British Museum* (London, 1892).

J. A. Knudtzon, *Die el-Amarna-Tafeln* [abbreviated as *EA*] (Leipzig, 1915).

W. F. Albright, in *ANET*, pp. 483–490.

3. HAZOR AND THE CONQUESTS OF JOSHUA

Y. Yadin and others, *Hazor*, Vol. I (1958); II (1960); III–IV, plates (1961).

Y. Yadin, 'Hazor' in D. Winton Thomas (ed.), *Archaeology and Old Testament Study* [abbreviated as *AOTS*] (Oxford, 1967), pp. 244–263.

4. THE PHILISTINES

Casts: A. H. Sayce: *The Races of the Old Testament* (London, 1925).
General: T. Dothan, 'The Philistines', *Antiquity and Survival* II (1957), pp. 151–64.
    W. Wreszinski, *Atlas der altägyptischen Kulturgeschichte II* (1936), pp. 29–30, s.v. *Nordvölker*.
    T. C. Mitchell, 'Philistia' in *AOTS*, pp. 404–427.
Sword: H. R. Hall, *Proceedings of the Society of Antiquaries*, XXXVII, pp. 127–30.
    H. R. Hall, *Aegean Archaeology* (London, 1915), pp. 247, 252.

5. CANAANITE CULT FIGURES

J. B. Pritchard, *Palestinian Figurines* (New Haven, 1943).

6. THE WISDOM OF AMENEMOPE

E. A. Wallis Budge, *Egyptian Hieratic Papyri in the British Museum*, 2nd series (1923), pp. 9–18, 41–5; pls. I–XIV.

E. A. Wallis Budge, 'The Precepts of Life, by Amen-em-apt, the son of Ka-nekht' in *Recueil des études égyptiennes* (Paris, 1922).

F. Ll. Griffith, 'The Teaching of Amenophis, the son of Kanakht', Papyrus B.M. 1074 in *Journal of Egyptian Archaeology*, Vol. 12 (1926), pp. 191–231.

D. C. Simpson, 'The Hebrew Book of Proverbs and the Teaching of Amenophis', in *Journal of Egyptian Archaeology*, Vol. 12 (1926), pp. 232–9.

J. A. Wilson, in *ANET*, pp. 421–4.

J. M. Plumley, in *DOTT*, pp. 172–186.

R. J. Williams, 'The Alleged Semitic Original of the Wisdom of Amenemope' in *Journal of Egyptian Archaeology*, Vol. 47 (1961), pp. 100–6.

B. J. Peterson, 'A New Fragment of *The Wisdom of Amenemope*', in *Journal of Egyptian Archaeology*, Vol. 52 (1966), pp. 120–128.

7. PASSING CHILDREN THROUGH THE FIRE OF MOLOCH

E. Dhorme, 'Le Dieu Baal et le Dieu Moloch', *Anatolian Studies*, VI (1956), pp. 57–61.

D. Harden, *The Phœnicians* (1962) pp. 94–101.

8. PHOENICIAN TRIBUTE

A. H. Layard, *Monuments of Nineveh* I (1849), pl. 40.

Sir E. A. W. Budge, *Assyrian Sculptures in the British Museum* (1914), pl. XXVIII.

C. J. Gadd, *The Stones of Assyria* (1936), pp. 137, 163

R. D. Barnett, *Assyrian Palace Reliefs* (1959), pl. 9.

H. R. Hall, *Babylonian and Assyrian Sculptures in the British Museum* (1928), pl. XXXIII, 1.

A. Paterson, *Assyrian Sculptures. Palace of Sinacherib* (1915), pl. 11.

N. Glueck, in *AOTS*, pp. 437–440.

9. THE IVORY HOUSE OF AHAB

J. W. and G. Crowfoot, *Samaria-Sebaste. Reports, 2. Early Ivories from Samaria.* (Palestine Exploration Fund, London, 1938.)

10. CHERUBIM AND THE TEMPLE OF SOLOMON

W. F. Albright, 'What Were the Cherubim?' *Biblical Archaeologist*, I (1938), pp. 1–3.

R. D. Barnett, *Catalogue of the Nimrud Ivories in the British Museum* (1957), pl. 1 and pp. 179–80.

11. SHALMANESER III (859–824 B.C.)

Text: Cuneiform (from Kurkh near Diyarbakir, South East Turkey): H. C.
Rawlinson, *Cuneiform Inscriptions of Western Asia*, III (1870), pls.7–8.
Translation: D. D. Luckenbill, *Ancient Records of Assyria and Babylonia*, I
(1926), § 595–611.
A. L. Oppenheim, in *ANET*, pp. 277–279.
Discovery: J. E. Taylor, *Journal of Royal Geographical Society*, XXXV
(1865), p. 21 ff. C. J. Gadd, *The Stones of Assyria* (1936), p. 125.

12. THE HOMAGE OF JEHU

Text: Cuneiform: A. H. Layard, *Inscriptions in the Cuneiform Character* (1851),
pp. 87–91.
Translation: A. L. Oppenheim, in *ANET*, pp. 278–81.
Discovery: A. H. Layard, *Nineveh and its Remains*, I (1849), pp. 346–8. See
C. J. Gadd, *The Stones of Assyria* (1936), pp. 48 and 147–8.

13. TIGLATH-PILESER III INVADES PALESTINE

R. D. Barnett and M. Falkner, *The Sculptures of Tiglath-pileser III* (1961),
pls. LXXX–LXXI. Relief 36, p. 30.

14. THE CAPTURE OF SAMARIA (722 B.C.)

Nimrud Prism (in Iraq Museum, Baghdad). C. J. Gadd, *Iraq*, XVI (1954),
pp. 173–201.
Relief: H. R. Hall, *Babylonian and Assyrian Sculpture in the British Museum*
(1928), pl. XXVII.

15. SENNACHERIB AND HEZEKIAH

D. D. Luckenbill, *Ancient Records of Assyria and Babylonia*, II (1927),
§ 239–41.
A. L. Oppenheim, in *ANET*, pp. 287–8, (91032), 301 (K. 1295).
R. F. Harper, *Assyrian and Babylonian Letters*, VI (1902), p. 683.
L. Waterman, *Royal Correspondence of the Assyrian Empire*, I (1930), p. 440.

16. THE SIEGE OF LACHISH

Reliefs: A. H. Layard, *Monuments of Nineveh*, II (1853), pl. 20–24
H. R. Hall, *Babylonian and Assyrian Sculptures in the British Museum* (Paris, 1928), pl. XXXVIII.
R. D. Barnett, 'The Siege of Lachish', *Israel Exploration Journal*, VIII (1958), pp. 161–164.
Cuneiform Text: (inscribed after 5th Campaign): D. D. Luckenbill, *Ancient Records of Assyria and Babylonia*, II (Chicago, 1927), p. 166, § 383.
Excavations: O. Tufnell, *Lachish III. The Iron Age* (London, 1953).

17. THE TOMB OF SHEBNA, A ROYAL STEWARD

C. Clermont-Ganneau, *P.E.F. Quarterly Statement* (1871), p. 103 and *Archaeological Researches in Palestine*, I (1889), p. 305 ff.
N. Avigad, 'The Epitaph of a Royal Steward from Silwan Village', *Israel Exploration Journal*, III (1953), pp. 137–52.

18. THE LACHISH LETTERS

H. Torczyner, *Lachish I. The Lachish Letters* (London, 1938).
D. Diringer, in O. Tufnell, *Lachish III*, pp. 331–39.
W. F. Albright, in *ANET*, pp. 212–17.
D. Winton Thomas, in *DOTT*, pp. 321–22.

19. THE END OF ASSYRIA, THE FALL OF NINEVEH, AND THE CAPTURE OF JERUSALEM

Babylonian Chronicle: D. J. Wiseman, *Chronicles of Chaldaean Kings* (London, 1956).
Carchemish: Sir C. L. Woolley, *British Museum Excavations at Carchemish*, Vol. II (1921), pl. 22 (arrowheads) and pl. 24 (shield); Sir C. L. Woolley and R. D. Barnett, Vol. III (1952), pp. 251–7.

20. THE ACCESSION OF CYRUS THE MEDE

Text: H. C. Rawlinson, *Cuneiform Inscriptions of Western Asia*, V (1880), pl. 35.
Transliteration and translation (German): F. H. Weissbach, *Die Keilinschriften der Achämeniden* (Leipzig, 1911), pp. 2 ff.
English: A. L. Oppenheim, in *ANET*, pp. 315–6 (from which the quotation on p. 77 is taken).

21. DARIUS, THE GREAT KING, AND THE PALACE OF SHUSHAN

Frieze: M. Dieulafoy, *L'Acropole de Suse* (Paris, 1893) pp. 280–97.
Seal: T. G. Pinches, *Journal of the British Archæological Association* (1885), pl. 3, 6, p. 11.
    J. Yoyotte, *Revue d'Assyriologie* XLVI (1952), pp. 165–167.

22. THE DEAD SEA SCROLLS

R. de Vaux, *L'Archéologie et les Manuscrits de la Mer Morte* (Schweich Lectures of the British Academy; London, 1959).
G. Vermes, *The Dead Sea Scrolls in English* (Pelican; Harmondsworth, 1962).

23. REMINISCENCES OF THE TEMPLE OF HEROD: THE OSSUARY OF NICANOR

C. Wilson and C. Warren, *The Recovery of Jerusalem* (1871), pp. 305, 493.
C. Clermont-Ganneau, *Revue archéologique*, 1873.
C. Clermont-Ganneau, *P.E.F. Quarterly Statement* (1903), pp. 125–31.
G. Dickson, *ibid*, pp. 93, 326–32.
R. D. Barnett, 'Reminiscences of Herod's Temple': *Christian News from Israel* (Jerusalem), XII (Oct. 1961), pp. 14–20.